COCKATIEL!
GUIDE FOR BEGINNER

Complete guide on everything
you need to kwon about
cockatiel: care, behavior,
housing, health, breed and
history

Laura Ivan

Table of Contents

CHAPTER ONE

INTRODUCTION

Cockatiels are little, peaked individuals from the parrot family. They are known for their smooth nature. Dim is the most widely recognized shading, yet they are likewise accessible in pearl, white-confronted, whitefaced pearl, lutino, pied and more shading variationsDiet You may see a layer of fine, white residue covering essentially everything close to your cockatiel's pen, particularly protests that draw dust with static, similar to the TV. This residue originates from white powder-down quills that develop near the winged animal's skin. These quills develop among the down plumes, and both are utilized to help protect the flying creature. What's remarkable about the powder down quills is that the tips disintegrate into a fine residue as the flying creature dresses, spreading the powder all through the plumes and assisting with waterproofing the fledgling.

The residue isn't an issue for a great many people, it can make respiratory issues and even exasperate asthma for other people. Cockatiels can cause unfavorably susceptible responses in other pet flying creatures kept in closeness; macaws appear to be particularly influenced by dustier flying creature species.

Washing your cockatiel every now and again decreases quill dust, and putting an air channel close to your winged animal's confine, similar to the HEPA channel, will clean the air and chop down the chance of respiratory issues. I have had numerous cockatiels throughout the years, and I never to such an extent as sniffled from the residue. Also, I'm not a habitual duster

An even cockatiel diet comprises of:

• Specialized pellets should make up 60 to 70% of diet, in addition to new vegetables and foods grown from the ground measures of invigorated seeds.

• Clean, new, separated, without chlorine water, changed day by day.

• Do not feed feathered creatures avocado, natural product seeds, chocolate, caffeine or liquor as these can cause genuine ailments. Keep away from sugar and high fat treats.

CHAPTER TWO

TAKING CARE OF YOUR COCKATIEL

Things to recollect when taking care of your cockatiel:

• Fresh food and water ought to consistently be accessible.

• Vegetables and natural products not eaten inside a couple of hours ought to be disposed of.

• Treats ought not surpass 10% of all out food.

• Cockatiels adjust well to average family unit temperatures, not to dip under 65°F or to surpass 80°F; be wary of outrageous temperature changes. The natural surroundings ought to be set off the floor in a region that is sufficiently bright and away from drafts.

• A environment around 24"W x 24"D x 30"H, with metal bars divided no more prominent than 1/2" separated, makes a decent home for The cockatiel is appropriate for open air aviary life. This flying creature is a nimble flyer and values being permitted to exploit this normal characteristic. It likewise will value being outside in acceptable climate, absorbing the daylight. Daylight is significant for a winged animal's general wellbeing. Since it is a genuinely accommodating winged creature, it does well in a huge aviary with other mild feathered creatures, for example, budgies, a few types of grass parakeets and a few assortments finches. Try not to house cockatiels with lovebirds or bigger parrots; the cockatiel can't guard itself against these more forceful birds.one cockatiel. It is ideal to give the biggest territory conceivable.

•   Perches ought to be in any event 5" long and 1/2" in width; an assortment of roost sizes to practice feet and help forestall joint pain is suggested.

• A metal mesh over the droppings plate will get the winged creature far from droppings; line the droppings plate with living space paper or proper substrate for simpler cleaning. To dodge tainting, don't put food or water compartments under roosts.

• Cockatiels can be kept alone to bond with pet parent or two by two to bond with one another. Various kinds of feathered creatures ought not be housed together.

- Birds ought to be mingled day by day by the pet parent.

CHAPTER THREE

BEHAVIOR

• Cockatiels are known for mirroring dreary sounds and clamors.

• Bond effectively with their human partners.

• Relatively calm flying creature. Preferable known for whistling capacity over for talking.

• Cockatiels that are parent-raised, yet additionally presented to standard human dealing with through weaning, develop to be tamer and preferred balanced over those that are totally handfed or parent-raised.

• Tamed winged creatures promptly adjust to new environmental factors and exercises – open ahead of schedule to every day exercises in your family unit just as to different pets

• Are clever, inquisitive, and effectively diverted with straightforward toys. They love to investigate their environmental factors

• Cockatiels are social and require customary connection with individuals so as to fulfill their amiable nature.

• Cockatiels may bond with people, confine mates, toys, or other pen goods. Romance, mating conduct and egg-laying normally result.

• Foraging stations, puzzle-feeders, and "occupied" toys give fundamental natural improvement and decrease the opportunity of quill picking, animosity, or different issues

• Birds with unhindered access in the home will experience various risks: suffocating, poison ingestion, electric shock, wounds, and so on. Cockatiels ought to be limited to their confine or housed in a "winged creature neighborly" safe room when not under direct management.

CHAPTER FOUR

NATURAL SURROUNDINGS MAINTENANCE

• Clean and sanitize the living space and roosts routinely with a 3% blanch arrangement; supplant substrate or living space liner week after week or all the more regularly varying.

• Replace roosts, dishes, and toys when worn or harmed; pivot new toys into the environment consistently.

• Ensure that there are no living space parts or toys with lead, zinc or toxic paints or aroused parts as these can cause genuine clinical issues whenever ingested by your winged animal.

• Do not utilize a great deal of cleaning operators around your winged animal as the exhaust can be unsafe. It is prescribed to utilize a characteristic cleaning item.

Preparing and Hygiene

• Provide separated, chlorinefree, tepid water consistently for washing; evacuate the water when done. As another option, fog the flying creature with water.

• Clipping flight plumes, when done accurately, can help forestall injury or getaway; counsel an avian veterinarian on what is best for your winged animal.

• Nails ought to be cut by a certified individual to forestall injury to the winged creature.

CHAPTER FIVE

INDICATIONS OF A HEALTHY COCKATIEL

- Active, alarm, and agreeable

- Eats and beverages for the duration of the day

- Dry nares and brilliant, dry eyes

- Beak, legs and feet typical in appearance

- Clean, dry vent

- Smooth, all around prepared plumes

Warnings

- beak expanding or gatherings

- fluffed, culled, or ruined plumes

- sitting on floor of living space

- wheezing or hacking

- runny or stained stools

- favoring one foot when not dozing

- eye or nasal release

- red or swollen eyes

- loss of hunger

Normal Health Issues

Wellbeing Issue Symptoms or Causes Suggested Action

Chlamydiosis Appetite misfortune, cushioned plumes, nasal release, lime green defecation, conjunctivitus. Seek prompt avian veterinary consideration.

Conjunctivitis Red eyes, tearing; shut, puffy eyes. Consult your veterinarian and wipe eyes with warm water.

Diarrhea Fecal part of stool not framed. various causes, from change in diet to inward parasites.

Consult your veterinarian and guarantee appropriate eating routine.

Egg-Laying Cockatiels

Most hens have the particular attitude to make more cockatiels, regardless of whether there's no male around. Visit egg laying is an issue in cockatiels, and however egg laying is organically natural, numerous female cockatiels will lay such a large number of eggs in short progression, causing potential medical problems, including egg authoritative, loss of motion, and debilitating of the bones.

Because she's laying eggs doesn't imply that your cockatiel needs or needs a mate or to have infants. It implies that her body has been imparted outside signs that it's an ideal opportunity to home, and she can't support her impulses. Normally, a cockatiel will come into mating condition when the light gets longer in the spring. A plenitude of food and water likewise prompts a cockatiel to need to set up house. Since you're not going to limit your fowl's food and water, confine the light your hen gets on the off chance that she continues laying eggs. Use sun lights as well as a pen spread to permit close to 10 hours of daylight daily until her hormones quiet down and she quits settling.

On the off chance that your fowl is laying and sitting on eggs, permit her to have them for a couple of days, and afterward expel them. It's not important to supplant the eggs with plastic eggs, the same number of canary raisers do. This will just draw out her sitting on them. Settling is exceptionally distressing for a female cockatiel without a male. Most matches alternate sitting on the eggs, so if she's distant from everyone else, she may swear off the food and water dish so as to ensure her eggs, regardless of whether they'll never bring forth.

CHAPTER SIX

COCKATIEL HISTORY

The first cockatiel – dim, an "Ordinary", is one of the 431 one of a kind local Australian feathered creatures, first portrayed in the last part of the 1700's.

There are numerous likenesses between the cockatiel and cockatoos, however since the cockatiel has some anatomical contrasts from the other seventeen individuals from the cockatoo family, the cockatiel has been ordered into its own virtuoso.

A sentimental researcher wasn't a long way from wrong in naming their stand-out Nymph(icus) in 1832, after a legendary request of excellent ladies who lived in the forested areas, knolls, waterways and mountains and trees and who served a more elevated level goddess. The grouped name inevitably became Nymphicus hollandicus, of the Cacatuidae (Cockatoo) family (before chromosome testing), the Nymphicinae subfamily, Nymphicus variety.

The name was streamlined from a more confounded Latin order to Hollanicus an understudy of characteristic history, in 1792. The cockatiel has been perceived by those in the past as the "Wonderful Maiden of New Holland." Cockatiels at that point got their own species name, HollandicusThe logical name experienced a few changes and varieties before a naturalist its current structure in 1832. The name makes an interpretation of truly into 'goddess of New Holland,' which is the name Australia was known by it.